Meditation

A Concise Handbook And Strategies For Reattaining A State Of Tranquility, Mindful Awareness, And Contentment

(Compendium On Synchronized Integrated Meditation Techniques & Relevant Protocols)

Ludovico Franzoni

TABLE OF CONTENT

Why Meditate? 1

Assuming Control Of Your Day 24

What Is The Number Of Existing Hypnosis Types, And What Are The Frequencies At Which They Operate? 35

The Five-Minute Meditations 43

Cognitive Processes 59

Chakras 73

Walking While In Meditation. 91

Requesting Attention To The Loaf Of Breadit Is Imperative To Consume Food On A Daily Basis. 97

Contemplative Breathing Exercise For Enhancing Mindfulness 110

How To Meditate? 157

Meditative Yoga Poses 171

Why Meditate?

Presently, there is a prevailing acknowledgement, substantiated by the outcomes of scholarly investigation, regarding the advantageous impacts that meditation imparts on both mental and physical well-being. This elucidates the burgeoning appeal of meditation in contemporary Western society, and the subsequent examination of the psychophysiological transformations linked to meditation will be addressed subsequently within this chapter. However, in a majority of Eastern nations where meditation is cultivated, and among numerous Western individuals who have adopted the practice, the primary focus remains on the traditional objective of attaining mystical experiences, rather than prioritizing the associated health advantages.

Mystical experience

The act of meditation has been employed as a method for the cultivation of spiritual growth for millennia. By engaging in the practice of meditation, one's consciousness undergoes a gradual refinement and expansion, leading to a profound comprehension of oneself and an enhanced perception of one's interconnectedness with the surrounding environment. The primary objective of meditative practice is to attain firsthand, experiential understanding of the fundamental essence of reality.

The fundamental truth perceived through mystical encounters is recognized under various designations. In philosophical discourse, ultimate or absolute reality is frequently denoted, whereas poets and visionaries occasionally allude to it as the One or the Truth. It represents the Taoist path, is cherished by Sufis, and embodies the Buddhist concept of emptiness. Christian mystics are acquainted with it as the Godhead, while followers of Hinduism refer to it as Brahman or the Self.

In the occurrence of a mystical encounter, any notion of 'self' and possessiveness evaporates. The consciousness of individuals converges into a state of pure and boundless existence. This state should not be misconstrued as confusion; rather, it is characterized by remarkable lucidity.

Numerous designations have been employed to characterize it - unadulterated existence, transcendent awareness, euphoric felicity, boundless affection, the amalgamation of contradictions, undivided 'suchness', and the like - however, these appellations and depictions impart scarce elucidation. As per the beliefs upheld by all mystics, the ascertainable truth can solely be apprehended through direct personal experience. Language is inherently insufficient to adequately convey this concept. Cognizant of the inherent constraints of linguistic expression, individuals of mystical inclination have resorted to the utilization of myths, metaphors, allegories, imagery, and paradoxes as means to effectively articulate their profound encounters and disseminate their erudition. Research conducted on these phenomena clearly indicates that the encounters of mystics throughout different eras and regions are fundamentally identical, notwithstanding potential variances in particulars and diverging interpretations. The primary aspect that every party emphasizes is the inherent unity and interconnectedness of all entities. This constitutes a dynamic union, perpetually in flux, constantly evolving, and consistently spontaneous.

Those who have had multiple encounters with the mystical realm never question the authenticity of their experiences. Even a fleeting glimpse of veracity can instigate a profound metamorphosis. The fundamental essence of mysticism resides in the direct encounter with reality and the subsequent cognition derived from it. The objective of meditation is to attain a state of being firmly grounded in this understanding, while the inner doctrine of all faiths and esoteric practices strives toward this same purpose.

Similarities between mysticism and modern physics

The perspective on reality that has arisen from recent advancements in physics is fundamentally akin to the one endorsed by mystics universally. The theories of relativity and quantum mechanics are collectively guiding us towards a comprehensive and interconnected perception of the nature of reality. This stands in marked divergence from the perspective of classical physics, which rests upon dualism and espouses a mechanistic understanding of the natural world. The ideas presented in this section may present an intellectual challenge for individuals with limited scientific expertise. However, the remarkable similarities between the experiential reality of mystics and the empirical reality elucidated by contemporary physicists are so pronounced, and their implications hold such significant weight within the realm of well-being and therapeutic practices, that disregarding them would be imprudent.

The model of the universe based on the Cartesian-Newtonian framework.

The intellectual traditions of Western society from the 17th century onwards have been significantly shaped by the contributions of the esteemed French philosopher, René Descartes, who is widely recognized as the pioneer of contemporary philosophy. Descartes, employing a method of profound skepticism, eventually reached the renowned proposition 'Cogito, ergo sum' or 'I think, therefore I exist'. From this declaration, he constructed his entire philosophical framework, categorizing consciousness and materiality as discrete entities that are wholly autonomous from one another. This phenomenon has prompted individuals in Western societies to primarily associate their sense of self with their cognitive faculties rather than encompassing their complete existence. This inclination stems from the prevalent perspective that regards the physical body as belonging solely to the realm of the material universe, thereby reducing it to a mere mechanistic entity. The repercussions of this dichotomous perspective have become readily evident within the realm of medicine.

The philosophical framework of Descartes's dualism, characterized by its mechanical interpretation of the natural world, exerted significant influence within the realm of scientific inquiry as well. It furnished the conceptual framework, formulated by the renowned English scientist Isaac Newton, that underlies the mechanistic portrayal of the cosmos and serves as the bedrock for the establishment of classical physics. The fundamental constituents (atoms) within the Newtonian conception of the cosmos consist of minute, rigid, imperishable particles that form the building blocks of all matter. In this framework, the entirety of physical phenomena is distilled to the motion, triggered by the gravitational force, of these particles across time and space in accordance with well-established principles of motion.

The Newtonian model enjoyed a profound status as the preeminent theory underpinning physical phenomena and serving as the foundation of scientific thought until the conclusion of the nineteenth century, when novel revelations surfaced, such as electric and magnetic phenomena, that eluded explanation within the confines of the mechanistic framework, thereby exposing its inherent limitations. Nevertheless, it was not until the remarkable scientific advancements of the early twentieth century that scientists were compelled to embrace a fundamentally disparate perception of reality.

Modern physics

The development of modern physics commences with the pioneering contributions of Einstein during the early years of the twentieth century. His initial significant accomplishment in the field of physics resided in his special theory of relativity. Based on this theory, time and space are posited to lack absoluteness and independence. They are inherently linked, constituting a continuum in four dimensions. One significant ramification of this observation is that mass is revealed to be merely a manifestation of energy.

Einstein's second significant contribution resided in a novel perspective towards electromagnetic phenomena. This has significantly contributed to the advancement of quantum theory, a theory that has fundamentally invalidated the traditional concept of physical solidity. According to the principles of quantum theory, the fundamental constituents of the universe do not consist of rigid, tangible particles as postulated in classical physics. Even at the subatomic level, such phenomena are fundamentally dissimilar. They are abstract entities that exhibit wave-like or particle-like characteristics, contingent upon our observational perspective. Subatomic particles are not discrete entities but rather intricate networks linking various elements, which in turn form intricate networks themselves. They lack definitive existence in particular locations, instead displaying inclinations towards existence. This implies that the physical entities prevalent in our daily existence exhibit, at the subatomic scale, a tendency to manifest as probabilistic wave-like phenomena. The solidity of matter emanates from the phenomenon that, when restricted within a limited volume, the electrons within an atom exhibit heightened velocities as they orbit the nucleus, thereby yielding the perception of the atom assuming a steadfast spherical form.

A vital aspect of quantum theory is that the properties of atomic phenomena are contingent upon the subjective awareness of the human observer. The manifestation of an electron as either a wave or a particle is contingent upon the interplay between the electron and the observer. The electron, in actuality, lacks any inherent properties that can be objectively measured or defined. Consequently, it can be concluded that the tenets of Cartesian dualism, positing that existence is comprised of two distinct and autonomous principles, namely the mind and matter, can no longer be sustained. The interdependence of the human mind and physical entities, as well as the inseparable bond between mankind and the natural world, are inextricably intertwined. We all share an interconnected existence.

Hence, the exploration of the atomic and subatomic realm serves to illustrate the interconnectedness, interrelation, and interdependence of the entire world. The components of matter are not separate entities per se, rather they are integral elements of an indivisible entirety that encompasses human consciousness as a fundamental component. Physicists have elucidated the inherent unity of the cosmos through the utilization of abstract mathematical equations and the indirect scrutiny of subatomic occurrences, employing exceptionally perceptive scientific apparatus. Mystics attain direct encounters with it during elevated levels of awareness achieved through profound meditation practices. The cognizance of this interconnectedness does not imply that mystics and physicists cease to acknowledge the distinctiveness of the objects and occurrences that manifest within the perceptible realm of our daily lives. It is primarily because they fail to perceive the divergences and disparities in the world as intrinsic aspects of reality.

Chapter 5: Extracting Additional Advantages

Meditation necessitates consistent dedication and unwavering determination. Engaging in this practice will gradually facilitate the reduction of your distracting thoughts, leading to the attainment of inner tranquility and a state of relaxation. Your mental state will experience a sense of openness and clarity, and you will attain a rejuvenating sensation as the uninterrupted stream of distracting thoughts is pacified through the practice of maintaining focus on the breath. You are advised to sustain this state of mental tranquility temporarily.

While breathing meditation serves as the initial phase of the meditative practice, it is worth noting that the act of breathing can possess an immense potency. Through the act of calming the mind, one can attain a state of internal tranquility and joy, free from reliance on external circumstances.

After the tempest of pessimistic thoughts wanes, a state of tranquility embraces the mind, granting passage to an innate and profound blissful serenity. This sense of satisfaction aids us in navigating the tasks and challenges inherent in our daily existence. One can alleviate stress by engaging in focused breathing exercises for a duration of ten to fifteen minutes on a daily basis. Your typical issues will dissipate. You will discover that handling difficult situations becomes more manageable. In addition, you will authentically experience a sense of warmth and benevolence towards yourself, fostering improved interpersonal connections.

In addition to experiencing a state of joy and tranquility, if you are observing or sensing these phenomena, it seems that meditation is proving to be effective for you.

Having Better Sleep

The expeditiousness with which you drift into slumber bestows upon you a greater duration of repose, thereby imbuing a heightened sense of restoration upon awakening. In addition, the practice of meditation enables one to effortlessly return to sleep upon experiencing episodes of awakening during the nocturnal hours.

Enhanced Cognitive Abilities

Difficulties can significantly amplify one's distress as they tend to overshadow rational thinking. Through the practice of meditation, one can cultivate the ability to think with clarity and actively explore innovative approaches to effectively resolve various challenges. The intellect commences generating novel and innovative concepts, thereby alleviating the tendency of fixating on recurring thoughts.

You Become More Productive

Not only will you perceive a heightened level of proficiency and expertise in your performance across various professional endeavors, but others will also begin to take note of these discernible advancements. Meditation has the potential to enhance one's productivity in a professional setting. You will ultimately complete your tasks ahead of schedule and achieve superior quality.

Acquiring a Slimmer Physique

Over time, through the practice of meditation, your physical well-being will gradually improve. Your vitality is heightened, and your physical weight is reduced. Consistent engagement in meditation has the potential to alleviate bodily discomfort and sensations of pain. Over time, you will begin to experience a rejuvenation like never before.

It addresses issues related to posture

Upon engaging in meditation, one shall promptly discern the gradual relaxation of distinct bodily regions, irrespective of minimal exertion. Additionally, it has the ability to effectively target a particular postural issue, thereby eliciting positive psychological and emotional effects.

Enhancing Consciousness in the Current Moment

You are truly advancing when you cease to excessively ruminate on the past or fret about the future. Each day, your satisfaction in awakening amplifies as your consciousness of events deepens. Participating in activities prevents the mind from becoming distracted or preoccupied. Additionally, one develops a heightened sense of self-awareness concerning their actions. On occasion, individuals may exhibit retrospective awareness of their behaviors, such as succumbing to frequent outbursts of anger or causing harm to others. They would eventually experience a sense of dissatisfaction and subsequently lament the loss of composure. Undeniably, this is an auspicious indication. Through the practice of meditation, one can cultivate a state of mind that enables the conscious selection of alternative responses, marked by enhanced creativity and greater overall benefit, particularly in specific circumstances.

Noticeable Changes in You

It can prove challenging to discern certain alterations within one's own being. Examining oneself from a personal standpoint is a challenging endeavor, yet discernible alterations may become perceptible to others.

At times, you may find yourself focusing on your failures rather than your accomplishments. When this occurs, you are inclined to overlook the advantageous transformations unfolding in your life. Meditation has proven to facilitate increased sociability and diminished impulsiveness among individuals. They exhibit an increased level of compassion and a greater willingness to pardon. Meditation cultivates increased levels of patience and fosters a greater capacity for empathy towards others.

While meditation may involve fluctuations, it is indeed indicative of progress when one experiences an increased sense of calmness in pursuit of self-betterment. It is a common occurrence to experience immense joy in the present moment, only to find oneself in a state of utter turmoil the subsequent day. The acquisition of meditation is not a competition. Simply navigate the current situation by finding your own path. It might require a considerable amount of time, thus it is pivotal to maintain fervor and steadfastness in the pursuit of attaining inner tranquility. Over time, you will increasingly discover a heightened ease in engaging in meditation regardless of the time of day.

Assuming Control Of Your Day

The Importance of Exercising Authority over Your Daily Routine

Are you driven to attain success in the pursuit of significant accomplishments? Given this circumstance, it is imperative to prioritize "achieving mastery over your day."

The manner in which you allocate your time holds no significance, provided that you decidedly refrain from purposefully instigating utter disorder in your life.

To say the least, I had minimal influence over the professional, personal, and physical aspects of my life. On a certain day, my business coach initiated a conversation with me, seeking information regarding the engagements I had undertaken the previous day. I informed her that my thoughts and actions were scattered and unfocused. Despite my efforts to recall any notable accomplishments from the previous day, my mind drew a blank. Or week. a week or month. Due to my lack of attention to the passage of time, I squandered countless months in purposeless pursuits and lacked a clear focus.

I found myself trapped in a state of stagnation, experiencing a form of emotional distress, and I lacked the knowledge on how to overcome it.

She imparted onto me valuable counsel, expressing the notion that "assuming command over one's day is essential in reclaiming the upper hand." Regrettably, it took me several years to fully appreciate and heed her sagacious guidance.

Allow me to inform you of this fact: it is possible to transition from a state of extreme distress to a state of absolute mastery over one's daily affairs within a rather limited span of time. However, it is necessary for you to conscientiously exert yourself. Once you begin allocating the necessary attention to each day, you will gradually embark on a journey towards embracing your potential and diligently pursuing the manifestation of your unique life vision.

In order to assist you in managing your daily activities, I would like to offer you seven valuable suggestions.

Guidance for Maximizing Productivity and Time Efficiency throughout the Day

1. Develop a comprehensive understanding of your objectives that you aim to accomplish by the culmination of the day – To assert authority over your daily routine, it is imperative to approach it with a determination to attain your aspirations and manifest your individual life

mission. It is vital to possess a distinct comprehension of your objectives for the day; without such clarity, one may easily find themselves meandering aimlessly, devoid of purpose or direction.

2. Establishing Specific Goals Once you have identified your desired outcomes, the subsequent phase involves ascertaining the daily actions necessary to achieve your goals. Establishing explicit goals allows you to delineate a path that will guide you from your current state to the desired future state.

3. Create a Strategic Implementation Strategy - After identifying your objectives, the subsequent phase entails devising a comprehensive approach for attaining them. Regardless of whether your goals are set on an annual, monthly, or weekly basis, it is imperative to adhere to a specific methodology and

execute the necessary actions in order to progress from point A to point B. These actions shall constitute your course of action. In order to exert dominion over your daily activities, it is imperative to possess a comprehensive understanding of the precise tasks that necessitate your attention on a day-to-day basis.

4. Schedule It – These are the words that my business coach would consistently emphasize: "If it is not included in your schedule, it will not materialize." Over the past 24 years, my existence has centered around my meticulously maintained schedule, which I associate with productivity, attending engagements, dedicating time outside of my abode, participating in conferences and workshops, traveling, arranging lodging accommodations, coordinating appointments, and experiencing a sense of pressure. The presence of my schedule caused considerable anxiety,

leading me to abstain from making any plans due to my negative feelings towards the factors that contributed to my state of burnout. Once you commence utilizing your calendar to organize the tasks required for attaining your objectives, you will begin to exercise greater authority over your daily activities and overall life. Direct your focus towards adopting productive habits.

5. Attain Surgical Precision in Your Objectives According to Robert Kiyosaki's insights on the interplay of concentration and accomplishment, it is advised to "Persist with a Singular Path until Triumph." Construct a meticulous strategic blueprint, subsequently execute it with precision, and allocate a specific timeframe for its execution. Subsequently, direct your focus toward the concrete implementation. On a daily basis, it is imperative for me to record

the "Daily Big Three" tasks as my planner possesses this functionality. There is an inherent interconnectedness between my action plan, goals, and overarching purpose. These three areas of concentration assist me in sustaining focused attention.

To effectively adapt to change, it is imperative to focus all of your energies on fostering the new, rather than indulging in futile resistance against the old. ~Socrates

6. Develop Beneficial Routines – Should you find yourself engaging in unproductive behaviors such as idly lounging, meandering without purpose, and convincing yourself of being trapped, recognize that this is merely a pattern of behavior. Establish beneficial habits. These are the routines that were cultivated prior to the onset of the tumultuous events that subsequently

disrupted the equilibrium of my life. Those patterns are extremely unpleasant. Consequently, I found myself deviating entirely from my original intended pathway. It will be imperative to modify one's routines in order to cease sedentary behavior and engage in physical activities. I have made the decision to commence a daily routine of embarking on morning walks consisting of 10,000 steps with the aim of enhancing my level of physical activity. I persisted in this endeavor for a consecutive period of 117 days, ultimately culminating in the establishment of a novel regimen and habit, while concurrently eradicating an unwanted routine and absence of structure. If one cultivates a consistent sequence of successful habits, one shall attain success. You cultivate regularity and steadfastness in your daily existence.

7. Stay informed about your progress. Attaining proficiency in managing your daily routine is not rooted in abstract principles reliant on subjective sentiments or emotional factors. You can accurately monitor your progress and assess the level of accomplishment you have made by establishing well-defined objectives and executing a systematic daily course of action. Consistently remain cognizant of your numerical data. This facilitates the evaluation of the effectiveness of your strategy and allows for identification of necessary modifications and adjustments. Without taking measurements, one cannot reasonably anticipate any enhancements.

Begin to Take Command of Your Day Today

To achieve success in attaining your goals, it is imperative to maintain absolute command over each passing day. The achievement of noteworthy goals in life necessitates adherence to self-discipline, purposeful conduct, and steadfast concentration. In due course, you will reach a stage where certain actions will be executed subconsciously if you deliberately establish habits that align with your intended course of action. However, to reach that point initially, one must commence their efforts.

According to popular belief, embarking on a journey spanning a thousand miles poses the greatest challenge at its inception. Traditional Chinese Wisdom

Assuming authority over your day commences by allocating a solitary instance and providing it with directives on its future course. You possess the capacity to determine the manner in which you allocate your time, and whether it is being utilized optimally or detrimental to your goals. Your eminence, the greatness that lies within you, your aspirations, and the visionary outlook you possess for your life are all factors that render it imperative to dedicate oneself to the mastery of each passing day.

What Is The Number Of Existing Hypnosis Types, And What Are The Frequencies At Which They Operate?

Over the course of recent years, various models or approaches have been employed within the realm of hypnosis, many of which have fallen out of favor as a result of the progressive advancements in neuroscience and psychotherapy. Similar to psychological therapies, hypnotherapy, too, is not unfamiliar with the tenets of scientific comprehension. In light of its proven inefficacy, the initial methods employed in hypnotherapy, which were predominantly founded on erroneous axioms, had to be invalidated.

What are the potential consequences if they employ outdated hypnosis techniques or utilize obsolete hypnotic frameworks? The primary consequence that arises from the utilization of antiquated forms of hypnosis is a notable lack of effectiveness. The implemented model lacks adequate clinical coping abilities to eradicate the disorder, as its framework aligns with axioms that have been deemed inappropriate by neurosciences. Alternatively, in different scenarios, the utilized structure may be antiquated to the extent that it exhibits deficiencies in terms of resolution and is additionally iatrogenic. The various techniques of hypnosis employed have consequential impacts on individuals' psychological well-being. Hence, it is imperative to closely examine the therapeutic approach employed, as it significantly relies on the hypnotist's abilities to induce extinction.

Over the course of the history of hypnosis, various methodologies and forms of hypnosis have been employed in order to elucidate its functioning, elucidate the influences and processes involved in hypnotherapy, and even delve into their potential impact on our behavioral patterns. In general, the evolution of these forms of hypnosis and theories has occurred in tandem with advancements in scientific understanding of neurosciences. There has seldom been a distinct lineage of hypnosis, but it has consistently been intertwined with psychology, albeit not always in the context of extended therapeutic interventions.

Whilst several forms of hypnosis that have been utilized since their inception are still in practice today, it is worth noting that behavioral therapies, including hypnotherapy, have perpetually undergone advancements, resulting in enhanced efficacy and a better understanding of the cognitive processes associated with it. The methods of hypnosis employed have additionally exhibited a degree of variation.

It is reasonable to suggest that a subsequent generation should supersede and eradicate the antiquated predecessors, based on sound reasoning and rational judgment. Hence, this would render it obsolete in favor of a new generation that is more advanced, productive, and possesses profound scientific acumen. Nevertheless, this assertion has not been corroborated in either the field of psychology or in the various modalities of hypnosis employed. Therefore, it is not unusual to come across therapists who employ both traditional first-generation therapy, which has been practiced for centuries, and more modern third-generation treatments, with hypnosis being the latest technique available. or mindfulness). This generates confusion among their clients, who tend to assume that the therapist serving them is up-to-date and uses the most efficient techniques available, which is not true at all.

First generation

Primarily, first-generation hypnotherapy encompasses those theoretical frameworks that employ abreaction techniques premised on the perceived correlation between trauma and the elicitation of psychological dysfunctions in individuals, thereby employing cathartic interventions or recollection of memories. Similarly, the practices of early behavioral orientations can be traced from Pavlov's classical conditioning methods to Skinner's operant conditioning techniques. Finally, eclectic techniques based only on metaphor and not on clinical procedures also enter this section. The clinical effectiveness of treatments in this era is at a rate of 11%.

Second Generation

Second-generation hypnotherapy is commonly defined as a framework in which cognitive-behavioral techniques are employed exclusively, with a specific emphasis on behavior modification techniques known as cognitive-behavioral techniques. This approach acknowledges the concept that distorted cognitions, if left unaddressed, can lead to psychological disorders (excluding those resulting from traumatic experiences). By utilizing cognitive techniques to restructure these distorted cognitions, a process referred to as modeling is applied. Furthermore, it considers the acquisition of unsuitable behavioral patterns (psychosocial and predisposing factors) that can be effectively approached by employing behavioral techniques like behavior modification, commonly referred to as shaping. The clinical efficacy of therapies in this current generation is demonstrated to be 81%.

Third generation.

Third generation hypnotherapy refers to the models that adopt a functional and contextual perspective regarding the psychological disorder (Mindfulness). Functional contextualism can be characterized as an orientation that encompasses comprehending psychological phenomena and their disorders, as well as examining the dynamic interplay between individuals and their surrounding environment. Third-generation therapies are founded on the principles of acknowledging the broader context and demonstrating a dedication to modifying these circumstances. The clinical effectiveness of treatments in this era is at an impressive rate of 80%.

Fourth generation

In the fourth iteration of this therapy, hypnosis and mindfulness have been excluded as mechanisms by which the treatment is delivered. Nonetheless, it is imbued with virtual reality through digital mechanisms, resulting in expedited and more effective psycho-therapeutic education compared to prior eras. This is owing to the complete captivation of attention facilitated by technology, and the swift acquisition of vicarious learning enabled by virtual reality.

The Five-Minute Meditations

In the following chapter, an extensive exploration will be conducted on the diverse array of five minute meditation techniques that are available for your experimentation. Kindly be advised that certain five minute meditation exercises can be utilized interchangeably, and it is not obligatory to strictly adhere to categorizing them in the manner delineated within this document.

It is often stated that the individual who rises early is able to secure advantageous opportunities. Indeed, it is accurate to assert that the early hours of the day are conducive to optimal meditation outcomes due to the heightened mental acuity experienced during that period. Let us explore several brief meditation techniques that can effectively initiate our day and prepare our minds for an elevated state of consciousness, fostering increased productivity and success in the professional environment.

A brief five-minute meditation suitable for beginning the day

First Step: It is crucial to ensure that during your morning meditation, your mind is clear and devoid of any traces of drowsiness or sluggishness. Hence, prior to consuming breakfast, it is imperative to gently douse your face with lukewarm water in order to achieve complete awakening. Next, proceed with a few stretching exercises to prepare yourself for the meditation session.

Second Step: As previously recommended, you may consider entering the room you have specifically designated as your meditation space, in order to achieve optimal outcomes. Assume a seated posture on a cushion placed on the floor or alternatively, opt for a chair, ensuring that your position entails the utmost comfort to endure a duration of five minutes.

Proceed to inhale and exhale in a natural and deep manner. It may be beneficial for you to engage in a silent internal dialogue, such as 'As I inhale, I am cognizant of the breath gracefully entering my corporeal form.' As I exhale, I am mindful of the departure of my breath from my physical vessel.

Step Four: Position your hand on your abdominal region and perceive the inherent ascension and descent of your abdomen during each respiration.

Step Five: Upon reaching the third or fourth inhalation, you will observe a discernible deepening and deceleration of your breath. Placing your hand over your abdominal region will instill a feeling of reassurance and protection. During this moment, it may be favorable to silently express sentiments such as 'As I inhale, I greet the forthcoming day with a smile.' Exhaling, I am aware that today holds the promise of greatness."

You will have the capacity to effortlessly accomplish this task each morning prior to commencing your work at the office. Furthermore, it will establish the ambiance for the remaining hours and stimulate your efficiency to an unmatched degree throughout the day!

You are not solely required to restrict the practice of meditation to the early hours of the morning. Indeed, you have the opportunity to partake in the same activities within the confines of the office, should you discover a spare moment amid your work obligations. Allow us to consider a suitable option for workplace settings.

A brief period of meditation lasting five minutes during scheduled intervals within the office setting.

Firstly, utilize the chair on which you predominantly remain seated throughout the day in your professional environment. Indeed, there is no necessity for you to vacate the vicinity where you dedicate the majority of your endeavors in order to engage in the practice of meditation.

Proceed to the second step: Take note of the number of breaths you take. Please shut your eyes and engage in the practice of silently enumerating your breaths. Please bear in mind that a single round encompasses a solitary act of inhalation followed by exhalation. Please ensure that you maintain the count following each exhalation.

Next, closely monitor your breath. It is imperative to either utilize a time application or establish a timer for the desired duration of your meditation, five minutes in this instance. This will prevent the occurrence of distractions arising from the incessant pondering on the elapsed duration of your meditation. It is imperative to engage in the process of counting one's breaths, as previously discussed.

Let us now explore an alternative five-minute meditation technique that can effectively be incorporated into the lunch hour.

A brief mindfulness session lasting five minutes that can be practiced during the midday break in a corporate setting.

First, establish a timer on your mobile device for a duration of five minutes, and then delicately shut your eyes.

Secondly, ensure that your feet are placed on the floor and maintain an upright posture while assuming a seated position in your respective chair. Place your hands gently upon your knees, ensuring that your palms are oriented towards the ceiling.

Proceed to the third step by gently closing your eyes and engaging in deep breathing exercises. Inhale slowly and deeply through your nostrils, allowing the breath to penetrate your lungs, while counting up to three. Inhale deeply while counting silently to three, then exhale gradually through your mouth, counting to three again and maintaining the exhalation for an additional three counts.

Fourth Step: It is crucial to maintain consistent practice of this exercise, ensuring that you inhale for a duration of three counts, hold your breath for three counts, and exhale for three counts, all the while holding the exhaled breath for three seconds.

Step Five: Upon activation of the alarm, inhale deeply through your nostrils thrice followed by exhaling through your mouth. Subsequently, proceed to gradually open your eyes.

There may arise occasions wherein you will be required to deliver a significant presentation. During such instances, it would be highly advantageous for you to engage in a brief five-minute meditation. This practice will assist you in attaining a state of mental equilibrium, thereby enabling you to convey your presentation with utmost competence. This entails utilizing the power of music as a tool for meditation, which will effectively tranquillize your mind unlike any other method, thus instilling you with enough enthusiasm to deliver your crucial presentation. Let us examine how we can guarantee this.

A Brief Meditation Practice prior to Board Presentations

First step: Connect a pair of headphones. Naturally, ensure that only the most serene music is chosen. You would prefer a genre of music that does not elicit overwhelming excitement or interfere with your ability to engage in a meditative state, such as hip-hop.

Secondly, it is advisable to adjust the music volume diligently, ensuring it is set at an appropriate level that prevents excessive distraction. Simultaneously, it is desirable to refrain from setting it at such a low level that one must actively concentrate on the music being performed.

Step Three: Ensure to maintain a natural and effortless breathing pattern. It is advisable to gently rest the tip of your tongue on the roof of your mouth as you proceed to breathe in deeply and gradually through your nostrils, subsequently exhaling through your slightly parted lips as opposed to exhaling through your nostrils.

Step Four: Periodically, you will observe the occurrence of thoughts in your mind.

Ensure that you redirect your focus to the music emanating in the vicinity. Indeed, the music demands such unwavering concentration that one must relinquish themselves entirely to its allure; it is imperative that every emotion is wholeheartedly invested in the sound, resulting in a profound enjoyment that penetrates to the very essence of one's being.

Step Five: As you permit yourself to align with the exquisite melodies resonating, you will discern the gradual harmonization of your respiration and cardiac rhythm with the melodic cadence. This signifies that you have attained the designated threshold referred to as the 'entrainment point'. Your emotional state is synchronizing with the music being performed and is progressing in an identical trajectory.

There may arise instances wherein one would need to manage significant conflicts within the professional setting. In such instances, it is quite effortless to be swept away by sentiments of exasperation and indignation, factors that can prove to be significant hindrances in the completion of a task. Allow us to examine a straightforward five-minute meditation technique that is capable of assisting us in reconciling our internal conflicts.

A Brief Five-Minute Meditation for Resolving Workplace Conflict

Firstly, you should gently close your eyes and allow those inner feelings of conflict to flow through your thoughts without imposing any form of judgment upon them.

Second Step: Cultivate a sense of benevolence and compassion, alongside profound appreciation for the present blessings you possess. Direct your attention to your breath, while maintaining a steady and composed mindset despite the tumultuous thoughts of anger or fear arising from the unresolved conflict within your consciousness.

Step Three: Cultivate an inner reservoir of love and compassion, allowing these sentiments to emanate from within, ultimately extending their reach towards individuals, including those entangled in conflicts. This will serve to prevent exacerbation of the current circumstances upon your emergence from the meditative state. This form of meditation that focuses on the experience of 'sensation' will facilitate the cultivation of an exceptionally impartial perspective, enabling you to make decisions based on the highest level of reason.

It is of paramount importance that upon your return from work, your mental state is fully relaxed. Otherwise, you will bear the burden of superfluous emotional strain from your professional environment into your personal sanctuary, which is unequivocally undesirable. This course of action would inevitably undermine your internal tranquility as well as that of the individuals you encounter at home. Allow us to examine a highly efficacious five-minute meditation technique that will enable you to relax and rejuvenate after your workday, thereby revitalizing you to thoroughly appreciate the remainder of your day. It can be accomplished with great efficacy, as one only needs to take a shower – an activity typically undertaken upon returning home from work, regardless.

Cognitive Processes

Cognitive processes refer to the ongoing mental processes or activities performed by the brain. In the aforementioned procedures, the cerebral faculties assimilate and analyze all incoming data originating from the external milieu. Let's say you are in the laundry room and you hear a big bang in the next room. You hastily rush over to discover that, while engaging in play within the confines of his bedroom, your child has inadvertently toppled his bedside lamp. Your heart is currently experiencing an increased pulse rate, prompting you to swiftly approach him to ensure his well-being.

Cognitive processes encompass various mental activities such as cognition, contemplation, assessment, recall, and analytical reasoning. They are the individuals who will have influenced your judgments in the aforementioned scenarios and shaped your subsequent actions. These processes leverage sophisticated cognitive abilities such as sensory perception, linguistic aptitude, imaginative processes, and strategic planning. It is imperative that they collaborate seamlessly in order to facilitate a comprehensive analysis of the situation and appropriately adjust to it. Hence, based on these interactions, we can effectively address the demands and challenges posed by our environment.

It is noteworthy to mention that while cognitive processes function harmoniously, they can also operate independently. For instance, an individual afflicted with a language disorder will retain accurate perception of stimuli and actively participate in problem-solving endeavors.

Cognitive Process Examination
Cognition is examined through diverse scientific perspectives such as

neurology, sociology, philosophy, anthropology, and linguistics. Cognitive psychology is the discipline within the broader field of psychology that focuses on the examination and analysis of cognitive processes.

A novel vantage point emerged during the 1960s, heralding a consequential shift in the prevailing philosophical framework. It precipitated the emergence of the cognitive revolution and fostered the investigation of cognitive phenomena. Presently, an extensive exploration is being conducted on psychological phenomena, with their practical utilization extending to nearly every facet of existence, encompassing domains such as sales and marketing.

Brain imaging, commonly referred to as neuroimaging, has proven to be invaluable throughout the entirety of this process. It has facilitated the enhancement of our comprehension regarding the mechanisms of information processing, and the discernment of the brain regions associated with distinct cognitive functions.

What is the Process of Cognitive Functioning?

The process of cognition initiates the transformation of sensory information. The sensory perceptions that you gather from your surroundings via your visual, auditory, gustatory, olfactory, tactile, and other sensory modalities are converted into signals that the brain can discern. This process facilitates the transformation of diverse information into signals that can be effectively processed by the human mind. As an illustration, when an object is propelled towards you, the visual senses will perceive this data and transmit it to the brain as a neural stimulus. Subsequently, your cognitive faculties will dispatch an indication to your musculature, enabling you to instinctively evade, thereby mitigating the risk of sustaining harm.

Additionally, the process of cognition serves to selectively extract pertinent sensory information, ensuring that only elements deemed personally significant are retained within one's awareness. The realm of human perception comprises an inexhaustible array of sensory encounters, with your faculties attuned to apprehending them in their entirety.

Nevertheless, it is unattainable to assimilate the entirety of these circumstances and derive significance from each individual one. Hence, it is imperative that the brain possesses the capability to selectively extract the essence of the material.

It is implausible to recollect every individual word or sentence that was uttered during the preceding lecture you participated in. Hence, the brain discerns essential notions and principles from the lecture which necessitate retention in order to comprehend the content expounded in the class. Your focus and retention in the course will be limited to the matters prioritized by your cognitive functions.

In addition to the act of condensing information to enhance its memorability, individuals also require the capacity to elaborate on said information during the process of its reconstruction. When recounting an incident to a companion that occurred a week prior, it is probable that while narrating the tale, you will gradually introduce embellishments or additional elements not present in the initial story in order to enhance its humor or entertainment value. This scenario could arise when attempting to retrieve the tally of items within your shopping list. It is plausible that you may include additional items that were not originally listed, but possess resemblances to some of the initially enumerated items.

This occurs in situations where an individual encounters difficulty in recollecting all the precise details associated with a specific occurrence. In situations where one experiences partial recollection of an event, the brain has a tendency to compensate for the missing information by selectively incorporating what seems to be relevant.

Cognitive processes are also beneficial for the retention and retrieval of information. The manner in which you recollect, the specific details retained in your memory, and the information that eludes your recollection, collectively serve as strong indications of the cognitive mechanisms at work within you. Certain individuals envision memory as analogous to a video camera that meticulously captures, categorizes, and archives various occurrences, preserving them for subsequent recollection. As per the findings of the conducted research, this process, nevertheless, exhibits a greater degree of intricacy.

In actuality, memory exhibits variability and possesses a degree of fallibility and fragility that is rather astonishing. For instance, the duration of short-term memory is limited to a relatively brief period of 20-30 seconds, whereas long-term memory is characterized by its enduring nature and stability, spanning years and even decades in some cases. Individuals have a natural inclination towards forgetfulness and the absorption of misinformation, both of which can distort their memories and result in the creation of deceitful recollections.

In conclusion, the manner in which cognitive processes operate has an impact on the utilization of information stored within the brain. Cognition encompasses not only the acquisition and retention of information, but also exerts a profound influence on mental processes and thoughts, thereby exerting a substantial impact on the choices and behaviors one adopts. It exerts influence on the degree of attentiveness you allocate to the surrounding environment, the precision and caliber of your recollections pertaining to past occurrences, facilitates comprehension of linguistic communication and operational mechanisms in the world, and facilitates resolution of any predicaments that may impinge upon your behavior and interactions with the immediate milieu.

Categories of Cognitive Processes "

Attention

A wide range of diverse stimuli is concurrently occurring in our vicinity. Nevertheless, individuals tend to direct their focus primarily towards the stimuli that captivate their interest the most. Certain activities, such as mastication and ambulation, demand minimal cognitive involvement, whereas activities involving verbal communication necessitate heightened concentration, particularly in situations where individuals are attentively engaged with your ideas. In any of these processes, the individual's capacity to direct his focus enables him to orient himself toward the stimuli that are pertinent to him, and subsequently, react to them.

Multiple types of attention can be observed, including focused attention, selective attention, arousal, sustained attention, divided attention, and alternating attention.

It is an advantageous circumstance that individuals are able to mechanize certain daily processes through repetition, thereby allowing for increased attention to be dedicated to additional tasks. For instance, in the initial stages of travel, as you acquaint yourself with the skill of driving, you maintain a vigilant focus on fulfilling your obligations, directing your complete attention towards this endeavor. Nonetheless, over time, the act of driving becomes instinctive, thereby obviating the need for excessive contemplation regarding one's actions.

Perception and Sensation

Various types of stimuli present in our surroundings give rise to sensory perceptions. The sensory stimulus must initially reach the sensory receptors, allowing the individual to discern and extract the pertinent information amidst the presence of numerous other sensory stimuli. Upon receipt of this information, one begins to perceive and interpret the stimulus.

On each occasion, you are utilizing your cognition, even in the absence of conscious awareness. As an illustration, one would be attuned to their posture, the gestures and activities of those nearby, the notifications received on their mobile device, sensory characteristics of food, and various other forms of stimuli. Experiences also serve as fundamental factors in shaping your interpretation of incoming stimuli. Gestalt psychologists held the predominant view regarding the potency of perception. Their contention was that as sentient entities, we perceive our surroundings holistically rather than as discrete components. They also demonstrated a substantial inclination towards comprehending the mechanisms underlying these different modes of perception, including illusions.

Memory

It is plausible that you recall the names of your elementary school educators; however, do you also happen to recollect the identity of your kindergarten instructor? Can you recall your closest companion from your elementary school years? Could you please inform me about the capital of Australia? What is the proper technique for performing on the saxophone? The responses to these inquiries and similar ones are intricately embedded within the recesses of your recollection. The cognitive faculty enables the accumulation and encoding of sensory information obtained from the surrounding context, amalgamating it comprehensively, and subsequently accessing it in the future.

There exists a variety of memory types, namely short-term memory, semantic memory, sensory memory, and working memory. These types of memories exhibit mutual interactions and collaboration, despite not being localized within identical cerebral regions. For example, a person who has suffered amentia will still remember how to cook, to walk, and can remember some people's names.

Memory is indispensable for the seamless execution of one's daily affairs. As a cognitive mechanism, it proves advantageous in the processes of encoding, storing, and retrieving information. Encoding is the process by which sensory stimuli are converted into a more coherent and manageable cognitive representation, thereby rendering it amenable for subsequent storage in the human brain. Storage refers to the temporal extent for which information remains retained within the neural structures of the brain. It also pertains to the type and quantity of information retained. Retrieval refers to the procedural operation of extracting stored information from its storage location and bringing it into conscious awareness.

Chakras

A Chakra is an inner locus of ethereal energy residing within the corporeal form. The energy centers play a vital role in the regulation of bodily functions, encompassing emotions, the immune system, organs, and all other intermediate processes.

Chakras possess the ability to experience blockages, resulting in the disturbance of energy equilibrium and its steady flow. Just as the circulatory system relies on the unhindered flow of blood through the veins, the equilibrium of prana, or life energy, plays a crucial role in maintaining the optimal functioning of both the mind and body. Any disturbance to the balance of prana can result in discomfort and have a detrimental impact on their overall well-being.

There exist a total of seven primary Chakras that necessitate your attention, and each individual Chakra assumes responsibility for its own distinct functions, alongside necessitating equilibrium with the remaining six Chakras.

This may appear quite intricate, however, in practicality, it is not. For the purpose of achieving optimal benefits from meditation, it is necessary to properly activate and harness the energy of your Chakras, thus utilizing the innate energetic potential of your body. Similar to the practice of meditation, the proficiency and efficiency of this skill increase with consistent practice.

The Chakras ascend in a vertical manner along the body, converging their energies into a primary energy flow referred to as the 'Sushumna'. This vital life force, referred to as (chi, prana), flows within our internal being, enveloping our external physique. From an external standpoint, this is commonly known as our Aura.

To facilitate your comprehension, consider envisioning the Sushumna as analogous to the intricate electrical circuitry within your physical being. According to traditional Eastern meditation practices, a vast number of subordinate energy flows, known as Nadis, is believed to manifest within the human body, approximately totaling 72,000. These Nadis stem from the primary central channel, Sushumna, and permeate throughout the body, intricately connecting with the various energy centers known as Chakras.

The Chakras undergo the process of opening and closing in accordance with the stimuli received from your emotional state. When individuals encounter a substantial amount of adverse sentiment, it is not uncommon for these emotions to often manifest as obstructions that impede the free flow of energy. By engaging in mindful contemplation, one can acquire the skills to regulate the flow of their energy, eliminate obstructions, activate and deactivate Chakras, and ultimately rebalance the body's inherent energy equilibrium.

Each of the Chakra points is denoted by an appointed color. In the process of activating the Chakra system, we initiate with the foundation Chakra and progress in an ascending manner up to the Crown Chakra.

The 4 Elements

Furthermore, alongside the 7 primary Chakras, the human energy field comprises the Physical Body, the Aura, the Hara, and the Spirit. The equilibrium of these four elements is imperative for optimal functioning of both the body and mind.

The Physical

This entity comprises all components of the corporeal form, encompassing delicate tissues, organs, the reproductive and digestive systems, and all intervening structures.

The Aura

The Aura is a combination of the energies of the seven major Chakras. Their collective forces create an effervescent aura that envelops the entire physique. This domain is vulnerable to the influence of your emotional and cognitive faculties, encompassing both conscious and subconscious elements. Individuals who have acquired the knowledge and ability to embrace the cosmic energy may intermittently perceive the Aura that envelops our beings. It manifests as a blurred hue that extends slightly beyond the confines of our corporeal form.

The Hara

The Hara represents a profound, impersonal energy source from which we draw upon to assist us in directing our attention towards our objectives. It is rooted in guidance and purpose, with a focus on achieving specific objectives. The Hara embodies the source of power that skilled martial artists harness in order to execute the impressive feat of breaking solid objects with their bare hands. It is the method employed by the monks in their detachment from physical suffering, yet it does not pertain to emotional anguish. We are unable to fully engage with the richness of life if we consistently possess unrestricted access to the Hara, as it lacks the presence of embodied emotions. It embodies sheer, unadulterated vitality. When we achieve a state of genuine inner equilibrium, we are able to tap into this energy as required and subsequently relinquish our grasp on it until its next anticipated demand.

The Spirit

The spirit epitomizes your very being. Attaining complete enlightenment is made possible through establishing a deep connection with the spiritual realm. It represents your utmost potential, your true essence. The human body serves as a vessel for the Spirit, enabling us to engage in interpersonal interactions within the realm of humanity.

The essence is experienced when an individual embraces us. It encompasses a pleasant and secure aura, inviting us to embrace and immerse ourselves in its soothing embrace. Love is the fundamental essence of the Spirit in its most pristine manifestation.

The 7 Chakras

Chakra One: The Foundation Chakra

This anatomical structure is located within the pelvic region and is symbolized by the hue of red.

It serves as the foundation of our physiological vitality and plays a pivotal role in our sustenance. It offers the necessary foundation for the preservation of our physiological processes, which are essential for our survival. This particular Chakra pertains to the preservation of our physical being and maintaining a sense of being rooted.

The Sacral Chakra exercises control over our adrenal glands, prostate gland, renal system, urinary bladder, and vertebral column.

Manifestations of blockages within the Root Chakra can be observed in the form of heightened aggression, feelings of insecurity, disturbances in psychological well-being, impaired sexual function, uncontrolled anger, disordered eating habits, and a sense of restlessness.

Hypertension and impotence are among the physiological complications linked to a restricted Root Chakra.

Sacral Chakra: The Second Chakra (Chakra of the Womb)

The Sacral region is positioned anatomically between the Naval and the Pelvis, and it is symbolized by the hue Orange.

We take great satisfaction in presenting Chakra to you, which symbolizes aspects of both sexuality, creativity, and reproduction. Energy traverses from the Root Chakra and ascends towards the Sacral Chakra.

The Sacral Chakra exercises dominion over our reproductive organs and lower extremities.

The manifestation of obstructions within the Sacral Chakra can manifest as behavioral patterns associated with addiction, intense devotion, an overwhelming sense of guilt and fear pertaining to experiencing pleasure and contentment, depressive tendencies, reliance on others to an unhealthy extent, episodes of heightened emotional sensitivity, diminished sexual desire, unquenchable and irrational cravings, as well as a dearth of innovation and artistic expression.

Physical obstruction can present itself in the forms of infertility, erectile dysfunction, gastrointestinal difficulties, lumbar discomfort, irregularities in menstrual cycles, renal infections, and urinary tract infections.

Third Chakra: The Manipura Chakra

This particular Chakra is situated in the region of the abdominal area and is symbolized by the hue of Yellow.

It pertains to our cognitive functioning, our conception of self, and our individuality. An obstructed third Chakra may induce a sense of unease regarding our identity and desires, while concurrently leading to a perception of limited self-mastery.

When the unrestricted flow of energy is channeled through this particular Chakra, it bestows upon us a profound sense of empowerment and mastery over our mental and physical faculties, thereby significantly enhancing our self-assurance.

The functioning of the Pancreas, stomach, liver, and gall-bladder is regulated by the Solar Plexus Chakra.

In the event of being obstructed, one shall encounter a dearth of lucidity, where matters appear solely in stark contrasts without allowance for any shades of gray, accompanied by a yearning for dominance over others, manipulative tendencies, absence of guidance, and the formulation of capricious plans lacking steadfast commitment for their execution.

Manifestations of an obstructed third Chakra encompass a range of physical indications such as disruptions in body weight, including both being underweight or overweight, neuropathic pain, diabetes, ailments affecting internal organs, digestive disturbances, respiratory complications, and the development of ulcers.

Chakra Four: The Chakra of the Heart

The Green color symbolizes this Chakra, which resides within the central region of our chest.

It symbolizes unfaltering affection, empathy, equilibrium, sentiments, and concord. Additionally, it represents the unification of our tangible existence with our elevated essence, our authentic nature, liberated from the external impact of our surroundings.

The Heart Chakra regulates the functioning of various vital organs and systems in our body, namely the thymus, heart, liver, lungs, and blood circulation.

An obstructed Heart Chakra will manifest signs of social anxiety, solitude, lack of trust in others, and tendency to criticize oneself and others.

Physical manifestations may encompass compromised blood flow and respiratory impairments.

Chakra Five: The Vishuddha Chakra,

Situated at the region of our throat lies this Chakra, symbolized by the hue of Blue.

This particular chakra is associated with veracity, self-articulation, interpersonal discourse, tactfulness, and erudition. If one ascends to a higher state of consciousness, this Chakra serves as a realm of profound wisdom.

The Throat Chakra assumes responsibility for the proper functioning of various physiological areas such as the Thyroid gland, throat, upper lungs, arms, and digestion.

An obstructed Throat Chakra will exhibit itself as a reluctance to voice opinions, introversion and apprehension in social situations, disconnection from both people and experiences, challenges in articulating thoughts, and unpredictable behavior and speech patterns.

Some potential physical manifestations of the condition encompass oral ulcers, inflamed throat, recurring headaches, thyroid dysfunction, neck discomfort, and larynx inflammation.

Chakra Six: The Chakra of the Third Eye

This particular Chakra can be found in close proximity to the Pituitary Gland, situated in the central region of the forehead, and is symbolized by the hue of Purple.

It exercises dominion over our intuition and imagination. It serves as the focal point for profound spiritual insight.

Once fully attuned, the Third Eye facilitates the dissolution of obstacles that separate the realm of the physical from that of the spiritual.

The Third Eye Chakra is associated with the Pituitary gland, the spine, the lower brain, the left eye, the nose, and the ears.

The manifestation of emotional disturbances resulting from a blocked Third Eye Chakra includes symptoms such as depression, anxiety, paranoia, and delusions.

Physical manifestations may include migraines, sciatica, seizures, sinus issues, and visual impairments.

The Seventh Chakra: The Chakra of the Crown

The location of the Crown Chakra is in proximity to the Pineal Gland, situated at the apex of the cranium, and is symbolized by the hue of White.

The Crown serves as the nucleus of our essence, the sanctum wherein we can attain enlightenment, complete spiritual consciousness, and sagacity through the alignment of our energy vibrations.

The Crown Chakra is responsible for regulating the functions of the Pineal gland, upper cerebral hemisphere, and right ocular organ.

An obstructed Crown Chakra can give rise to difficulties such as profound solitude stemming from an incapacity to establish meaningful connections with others, a sense of spiritual detachment, impaired capacity for strategic thinking and planning, and a dearth of purpose or guidance.

Physical manifestations may encompass symptoms such as neuralgia, migraines, psychosis, sleeplessness, melancholia, and neurological impairments.

Walking While In Meditation.

Engaging in physical activity rejuvenates the body, effectively shapes its form, instills a sense of tranquility, and prepares one for forthcoming endeavors. Once the exercises have been thoroughly mastered, they can be effectively implemented in challenging scenarios, including difficult conversations, examinations, dental appointments, and similar circumstances. It is suggested that athletes engage in walking meditation prior to undertaking intense training sessions (which entail greater exertion) as well as before competitive events.

The distinctive characteristic of this physical activity lies in the fact that with a rigorous execution of walking, it offers a dual benefit of promoting both meditative practice and cardiovascular exercise.

1. Demonstrate an improvement in speed over the course of two weeks, while maintaining proper posture by keeping the torso aligned and executing fluid hand movements. In addition, adopt a technique similar to race walking, characterized by wider pelvis movements. The foot is initially grounded by the heel, after which a rolling motion ensues, ultimately transitioning to the toes. The cadence of the motion exhibits vitality. Engage in physical activity for a duration of 15 to 20 minutes on a daily basis.

2. During the upcoming week, it is recommended to engage in a breathing exercise known as diaphragmatic-abdominal breathing. Engage in the activity of assuming a standing position, with your feet positioned slightly closer

together than the width of your shoulders. During the inhalation, maintain an abdominal distention accompanied by an expanded and slightly elevated chest. Ensure that the shoulders are not being subjected to undue tension. After completing the inhalation, one should experience a sense of fullness caused by the intake of air. Retain the breath within the lungs for a brief duration of approximately 2 to 3 seconds, following which, proceed to exhale. When expelling air, start by firmly depressing and compacting the chest, followed by the contraction of the abdominal muscles, creating an almost complete contact between its wall and the back. After a short intermission subsequent to exhalation, the cycle of respiration recommences. Engage in each exercise on a frequency of 5-7 sessions per week, allocating 15-20 minutes per session, which aligns with the duration previously dedicated to the mastery of brisk, unrestricted walking.

3. Now, it is imperative that you acquire the proficiency in harmonizing a swift, unencumbered gait with the practice of diaphragmatic-abdominal respiration. Inhale and exhale in a synchronized manner, aligning your breath with each individual stride. To commence, it is necessary to mention the following procedure: perform six inhalations, follow with a half-step pause, proceed to exhale for a duration of six steps, and then pause once again for two steps. It is preferable to take into account the quantity of steps. Inevitably, notions will manifest, yet you shall promptly proceed to gauge your progress and resume your respiration. Engage in physical activity for a duration of 15 to 20 minutes, ideally on 5 to 7 occasions during the week.

4. Once proficient in correctly executing the integration of an optimal range and employing the diaphragmatic-abdominal breath mechanics, proceed to progressively extend the duration of the respiratory cycle as follows: inhale for a span of 8 steps, momentarily suspend for 4 steps, exhale for 8 steps, and once again pause for 4 steps. Subsequently, proceed to replicate and prolong the respiratory cycle. Conduct an observational inquiry into adopting a brisk walking pace, while analyzing the correlation between the number of steps taken and corresponding respiratory movements, in order to ascertain the optimal health benefits.

5. Systemically augment the duration to encompass a 30-minute stroll, and extend further if temporal constraints allow. Prior to proceeding, it is advisable to carefully analyze your route and ensure the avoidance of any obstacles,

such as tree roots, that may disrupt your stride or flow. It is likewise advisable to refrain from crossing roads among moving vehicles, as your attention devoted to your breathing can inhibit your ability to exercise adequate caution in relation to vehicular traffic. Furthermore, it is crucial to allocate a minimum of one and a half hours between meals and physical activity. Engaging in morning meditation while on an empty stomach can prove to be highly beneficial.

Requesting Attention To The Loaf Of Breadit Is Imperative To Consume Food On A Daily Basis.

This leads us to the subsequent issue, trial, prospect, or extraordinary occurrence in unlocking the solution. "Grant us sustenance for each passing day" (Matthew 6:11, King James Version). This pertains to the process of addressing feelings of guilt and shame associated with our self-identity, ultimately asserting control over our own personal power.

We frequently find ourselves culpable of relinquishing our authority. Indeed, guilt pertains to an action that has been committed. Shame pertains to the essence of our personal identity as manifested through our actions. In the context of battle, a member of the armed forces may engage in combat and subsequently experience remorse for the act of causing harm to an adversary. Nevertheless, should he perceive himself as a perpetrator of homicide, he regards his selfhood as impious (aligned with a moral code). It entails a distressing weight of disgrace.

We require vitality, sustenance, and fortitude. We humbly request and diligently pursue the divine sustenance bestowed by the Almighty. We derive sustenance from the written word; we derive sustenance from the purifying influence of the Holy Spirit. Our purposeful endeavor is to partake from the source of unvarnished truth that nourishes and revitalizes the essence of our being. There exists an internal source that yields an abundant supply of vitalizing aqua. Within the span of our awakened moments, we nourish the intellect. Paul instructed, "In conclusion, my fellow brethren, focus your thoughts on anything that embodies truth, honesty, justice, purity, beauty, and goodness, as well as any acts of virtue and praise" (Philippians 4:8 KJV).

We carefully avoid indulging in loaves of bread and harboring impious thoughts. This practice exemplifies the art of contemplation in action, as it involves deliberately shutting the door on detrimental influences and refusing them entry into our consciousness. This constitutes a routine task performed on a daily basis. It is a challenging situation characterized by an abundance of negativity that we have started to internalize and derive sustenance from.

The indulgence in negativity impedes the ability to extend forgiveness. This does not imply that we fail to recognize the malevolence and pessimism that we encounter. It is not conducive for us to adopt an ostrich-like approach. Refrain from permitting negativity to nourish your spirit.

Jesus proclaimed, "Upon the departure of malevolent spirits from individuals, they venture into the arid wilderness in pursuit of repose, yet falter in their quest." Subsequently, it is stated, 'I shall retrace my steps towards my original source.' Consequently, it retraces its path and discovers the dwelling it initially emanated from to be devoid of occupants, meticulously tidied, and arranged in an orderly fashion. Subsequently, the spirit proceeds to encounter seven additional spirits of greater malevolence, ultimately infiltrating and establishing residency within the individual. Consequently, the individual is in a more disadvantageous position than they were previously. "That shall indeed characterize the encounter of this malevolent era" (Matthew 12:43-45 NLT).

The statement made by Paul in Ephesians 6:13 KJV, implies the necessity of acquiring the complete protection and strength provided by the armor of God. This alludes to the existence of a spiritual battle or conflict. It becomes particularly challenging when one is endeavouring to groom oneself. Particularly when engaging in the practice of meditation. Frequently, we desire expeditious outcomes for our endeavors; nonetheless, it is within the divine knowledge to determine our state of preparedness. It is imperative that we persist in our self-improvement endeavors, exhibit patience, embrace the benevolence of the divine, and bestow it upon our fellow beings. The author of the psalm expressed, "..he consistently reflects upon and contemplates his law throughout the entirety of the day and night" (Psalms 1:2 KJV). I once heard a learned individual proclaim, "If one possesses the opportunity to inhale and exhale, one possesses the opportunity to engage in meditative practice."

By abstaining from indulging in negativity, we fortify ourselves against succumbing to temptation. By refusing to let negativity nourish our spirits and instead embracing the nourishment of positivity, we can aspire to exemplify the qualities of Reverend as a prominent leader. Dr. Martin Luther King, Jr., akin to Mahatma Gandhi and in a similar vein as Malcolm X during his transformative phase. We come to realize and understand our true identity as offspring of the Divine; crafted in the very semblance and representation of God.

We acknowledge the truth that each of us has transgressed; each of us has engaged in acts that have deviated from what is considered moral and virtuous. We acknowledge the inevitable presence of the seven cardinal vices (pride, avarice, lust, envy, gluttony, wrath, and sloth) that persistently seek entry into our lives. Nevertheless, the practice of meditation can aid in perceiving its arrival.

The Lord's Prayer is nourishment for the spirit. It possesses the capability to eradicate the seven malevolent entities that take shelter within the depths of the human psyche. In the realm of the human psyche, specifically our basal cognitive faculties, we have the capacity to engage in daily exercises aimed at redirecting our thoughts towards honesty whenever they tend to veer towards deceitfulness. When the mind is drawn towards engaging in unjust actions, it is imperative for us to practice justice. When the mind inclines towards impurity, it is within our capacity to uphold purity. The daily sustenance of God's teachings enables us to boldly assert reality in the face of authority. It imparts the fortitude necessary to endure. The emergence of our identity, as children of God, fashioned in the likeness and image of God, starts to become apparent.

It is widely recognized among neuroscientists that the solar plexus functions as a secondary cognitive center within the human body. In accordance with the wisdom passed down by our forefathers, it was often uttered, "The stomach possesses its own consciousness."

The color yellow is associated with the third chakra, also known as the Solar Plexus. We have been informed of the phrase 'yellow belly' being employed to designate an individual who exhibits a deficiency in fortitude, valor, and audacity. The primary emphasis of this chakra pertains to harnessing one's individual power and sense of self.

We consume food in order to obtain essential nutrients and bolster our physical stamina. We require substance in order to facilitate our actions. The transgressions we commit, which deviate from our ethical framework, instigate feelings of shame and self-disappointment.

I have rendered pastoral support to numerous Veterans afflicted with Post Traumatic Stress Disorder [PTSD] who have expressed experiencing profound recollections and enduring physical and physiological responses to the remorse and shame associated with the exertion of their individual authority to cause harm, as well as witnessing the loss of life in others. The resolution of this deadlock lies in acknowledging that this represents a distinct part of the human experience.

The Throat chakra, also known as the fifth chakra, contributes to the process of healing by empowering individuals to express their genuine emotions and self-perception in an honest manner.

The Hermetic Principle of Rhythm aids individuals in achieving equilibrium by conscientiously aligning their moral compass in the opposite direction and in equal proportion. The equilibrium of life is discovered amidst the oscillation of our fortunes. An excessive consumption of bread poses health risks, just as insufficient intake of bread can also be detrimental to one's health. Life is replete with crests and troughs. We each require the ethical and metaphysical fortitude to triumph.

The fourth chakra, known as the Heart, is responsible for facilitating the purification of the solar plexus through the power of unconditional love. This occurs as we recognize and fully embrace our inherent divinity, in parallel to our acknowledgement of our inclination towards immorality through our earthly thoughts and desires.

The oscillation of the pendulum is an inherent truth of existence. We, as beings of the terrestrial realm, possess a corporeal intellect. We are individuals bestowed with the divine essence of God, guided by the virtuous nature of Christ. We oscillate between these two states throughout our entire lifespan. There exists an additional dimension in which a self-contradiction seems apparent. At this particular juncture in the Lord's Prayer, the paradox lies not in the act of obstructing negative thoughts or negative emotions, but rather in granting them permission to persist as they enter the sacred space (contemplative chamber). To adhere to the scripture, "Resist the devil, and he shall flee from you" (James 4:7 KJV) implies the act of refraining from associating any form of contemplation or evaluation to the presence within the premises or the impending entrance during the state of introspection.

Enable yourself to experience a range of emotions, be it sorrow, resentment, apprehension, trauma, animosity, personal weaknesses, or distressing recollections from prior events, without restraint. Simply engage in observation without passing judgment, and as you continue to do so, it will eventually come to an end. Through refraining from taking any immediate action, one becomes cognizant of the inherent essence and even the source from which it originates. You will understand it. Over time, its influence wanes and the negative aspects assume the impotence of a mere facade.

We have been created in the image and likeness of the divine. According to the Wisdom of Solomon 2:23 in the Apocrypha, as translated in the New English Bible, it is stated that "God fashioned man for everlasting life and made him the reflection of his own eternal nature." It is through this reflection and resemblance that we obtain a true understanding of our authentic identity. It aids us in maintaining composure amidst adversity.

The author of the psalm conveyed the message, "Remain calm and acknowledge my divine presence" (Psalms 46:10, King James Version). The concept of image identity and likeness identity (or our Christ identity) bestows upon us personal empowerment and fortitude. Upon contemplation, it becomes apparent to me that the fractured corporeal vessel and the spilt crimson essence of Christ, when examined at a profound level, bear resemblance to the visage and embodiment of the divine entity. Upon transcending the ethereal realms and entering this terrestrial plane, we perceive our existence as dichotomous, fragmented into two halves.

Contemplative Breathing Exercise For Enhancing Mindfulness

Mindfulness breath meditation proves to be efficacious in alleviating stress due to its ability to direct the mind's attention towards the breath. This shift in focus, away from multiple stimuli and towards a singular point, diminishes hyperactivity and induces slower brainwave patterns. Consequently, this transition facilitates the cultivation of profound awareness, intuition, tranquility, and overall improved state of wellbeing, as previously mentioned.

How to

Below, I present a formal guide on how to engage in this particular form of meditation with the intention of seeking alleviation from stress and anxiety, as well as fostering an increased level of concentration, mindfulness, self-perception, and overall state of welfare.

Step 1

To engage in meditation, regardless of the chosen technique, the initial step entails creating a conducive environment. For an individual who is entirely inexperienced in meditation, this generally refers to a serene and tranquil space or location. As your concentration and deliberate awareness broaden, so too will you acquire the capacity to disregard diversions. For the interim, it would be most advantageous to foster a tranquil space intended for meditation, specifically one that is devoid of assorted sources of diversion. It is not necessary for it to be elaborate; a peaceful corner is truly sufficient.

Additionally, it is crucial to determine both the timing and duration of your meditation practice. One can engage in meditation, both in the mentioned manner and through alternative methodologies, at any given moment. However, due to the fact that the advantages gained from meditation are contingent upon regularity, it is highly recommended to designate a specific time and adhere to it consistently, thereby fostering the establishment of a habitual practice.

When considering the length of your meditation sessions, it is recommended to commence with brief meditative periods ranging from 2 to 15 minutes, gradually progressing from that point onwards. Meditation entails practicing focused attention, a cognitive exercise that enhances the ability to engage in longer periods of meditation.

Preschedule meditation sessions into your daily life schedule so that you stick to the practice

Step 2

After accessing your designated space for meditation, the subsequent course of action entails assuming a posture of comfort either by sitting or reclining. Certain individuals engage in the practice of meditation while assuming yoga postures such as the lotus, half lotus, or the Burmese pose. Should individuals have the inclination to assume a particular posture, whether it be sitting or reclining in a prescribed manner, they are permitted to do so, as meditation primarily requires one to be mindful of attaining a position that is both comfortable and conducive to relaxation.

If you opt for assuming a particular posture, ensure that your spinal column remains aligned, yet not overly stiff; maintain a relaxed and comfortable resting position for your hands, and maintain a gentle, unfocused gaze. You may choose to either close or keep your eyes open.

Step 3

Ensure that your timer is appropriately configured to an optimal duration, and allocate a brief interval to cultivate an attentive awareness of your mental and physical state. Pause to establish a connection with your own being, and internally affirm, 'I am fully present in this instant.' By undertaking this exercise, you will reestablish a mindful connection with the present moment, priming your mind for the shift from the beta state of consciousness to a more profound and relaxed state such as alpha, theta, or delta.

Next, redirect your focus towards your breath; perform a series of deep breaths (approximately five deep breaths will suffice), being mindful of the act of inhaling and exhaling through this manner.

After completing your fifth deep breath, allow your breathing to return to its regular pace and redirect your attention towards mindfully observing and fully exploring every aspect of it with a genuine sense of interest.

What is your perception of the sensation during inhalation and in what specific area of your body do you predominantly perceive it? Are you able to perceive its movement as it enters through your nostrils, traverses your airway, and eventually reaches your chest, abdomen, and ultimately the lungs? Would you be able to discern the exact point at which the inhalation transitions into an exhalation that subsequently exits the lungs, traverses the air passages, and eventually emerges as warm air through the mouth or nostrils?

Mindfulness breath meditation pertains to embodying a state of being that centers around the act of mindful breathing. The greater extent to which you engage in the practice of attentively focusing on the breath, the more profound your level of mindfulness becomes, subsequently resulting in heightened effects of meditation on your overall levels of stress, anxiety, and feelings of happiness and well-being.

Step 4

The fundamental concept underlying this particular form of meditation is to maintain a state of mind that is fully cognizant of the ongoing nature of the inhalation and exhalation, occurring solely in the immediate present. As you engage in the exercise of directing and focusing your mental and conscious faculties in this manner, your attention will inevitably stray from the act of observing the breath. This is normal.

Upon perceiving the occurrence, kindly recognize this matter (and yourself for perceiving it) and promptly redirect your deliberate awareness towards the breath. By consistently acknowledging and redirecting the wandering of your mind, you will expedite the enhancement of your focus, attention, and awareness.

Despite the apparent simplicity of this meditation technique, its impact on one's state of being is immeasurable. Engaging in this form of meditation cultivates inner tranquility, enhances connectivity, amplifies self-regulation, improves concentration, heightens self-awareness, contributes to enhanced wellbeing, and fosters a profound sense of serenity towards existence.

NOTE: Most of the other types of meditation we shall discuss from this point on shall be succinct because in truth, once you internalize mindfulness breath meditation, you can easily integrate other types of meditation into your practice. The different forms of meditations we will proceed to examine will each make reference to this particular form of meditation.

Secondly, the Practice of Mindful Body Awareness Meditation

This form of meditation bears great resemblance to the mindfulness breath meditation discourse previously discussed.

The main distinction between this particular meditation technique and mindfulness breath meditation lies in the emphasis placed on different aspects. While mindfulness breath meditation primarily focuses on the breath, this specific approach directs attention towards systematically scanning different areas of the body. The goal is to use the act of conscious breathing to induce relaxation in these specific body regions.

This specific meditation technique proves efficacious in combating stress and anxiety. By attentively examining each body part and subsequently directing breath towards it, one can mentally envision the out-breath carrying away all the previously accumulated stress and anxiety specific to that particular body part. This process engenders a profound sense of tranquility within both the body and the mind.

How to

Herein lies a guide on engaging in the practice of body scan meditation, a technique that offers stress and anxiety alleviation, and contributes to the enhancement of overall well-being and contentment.

Step 1

Employ the previously mentioned technique of mindfulness meditation in order to establish a profound connection with your breath and physical sensations. To achieve a greater sense of groundedness and tranquility, engage in the practice of breath mindfulness meditation for a brief duration.

Step 2

Direct your focus towards your body and initiate a thorough examination; you may choose to commence from the toes or the crown of the head, depending on your personal preference.

The idea here is to move up—or down depending on which end you start with—scanning each individual part of the body. As an illustration, in the event that you have commenced from the toe region, you would fully engage in the act of observing the toes.

You would inhale deeply, being mindful of any sensations, tensions, or stress in those areas, and as you exhale, envision all the accumulated tension and stress dissipating from the toes, ultimately leaving them in a state of complete relaxation. Following that, one would progress upward, targeting the ankles, shins, knees, thighs, torso, and so forth. until you ultimately conduct a comprehensive scan of the entire body.

Step 3

In accordance with the conventional practice observed in the majority, if not all, forms of meditation, when the mind deviates from its intended focus, which it has a tendency to do in different ways, the objective is to redirect it towards the originally intended target, which, in this particular instance, involves directing one's attention back to the specific region of the body that was being scanned prior to the mind's diversion.

Regularly engaging in this meditation practice carries the potential to augment one's overall state of relaxation, cultivate a heightened sense of bodily and mental awareness, diminish the effects of stress and anxiety, and foster a sense of well-being and happiness through the inclusion of visualization techniques aimed at visualizing the departure of stress and tension from various parts of the body.

Mental Benefits

As previously mentioned, meditation has the effect of reducing anxiety and stress levels, enabling individuals to maintain a state of contentment and resilience regardless of challenging circumstances that may arise. Another advantage of maintaining a state of low stress is that individuals who do so tend to exhibit superior performance in high-pressure circumstances compared to their counterparts. This confers upon you a notable edge in various domains, be it athletics, commerce, governance, or even within your own familial sphere. You will maintain a composed demeanor and excel during each phase, ultimately attaining success in your life pursuits. Have you ever pondered upon the paradoxical phenomenon wherein even though a 100 meter sprint is fiercely competitive and the margin of victory is minuscule, certain athletes consistently emerge victorious in every single sprint? This is primarily attributed to their composed demeanor prior to, during, and subsequent to the sprint, which is frequently attributed to the regular practice of meditation.

The business scenario exhibits a parallel phenomenon. Prominent global business leaders engage in the practice of meditation, which empowers them to consistently perform at a high level and remain at the pinnacle of their success.

Additionally, the practice of meditation enhances an individual's emotional equilibrium, consequently allowing one to maintain a state of serenity and composure throughout various stages of life. You would have the opportunity to cultivate meaningful connections with those in your vicinity and experience a gratifying existence. Moreover, individuals who exhibit emotional stability are capable of deriving utmost satisfaction from all aspects of their life, be it their familial obligations, social interactions, professional pursuits, or athletic endeavors. By maintaining emotional equilibrium, one can effectively evaluate the advantages and disadvantages of a given situation, thereby enabling sound decision-making in all aspects of life.

It is an uncommon occurrence to encounter individuals who possess emotional stability, and those who do will invariably be positioned at the pinnacle of success. Indeed, due to their unwavering emotional equilibrium, they consistently demonstrate sound judgement, which consequently places them amongst the ranks of accomplished individuals. And when I refer to success, I am not necessarily alluding to the possession of a Fortune 500 company, but rather the achievement of favorable outcomes in relationships, financial matters, health, and overall lifestyle management.

One additional benefit of meditation is that it enhances one's ability to regularly generate innovative concepts. Can you provide speculation as to the reason behind this phenomenon? The explanation is rather straightforward as the mind is free from clutter. In our contemporary society, we find ourselves burdened by an overwhelming level of stress on a daily basis, stemming from various aspects of our lives such as professional obligations, familial dynamics, interpersonal relationships, and even recreational activities, among others. Through the diligent practice of meditation, individuals can effectively declutter their mental space and enhance their ability to concentrate on the task at hand in an optimal manner. Maintaining a steadfast focus cultivates ingenuity, consequently fostering an enhanced sense of creativity as one consistently engages in the practice of meditation.

Furthermore, it is widely understood that cultivating a creative mindset inevitably results in heightened levels of productivity, thereby contributing significantly to attaining success across various domains. Consequently, this constitutes another significant advantage of engaging in meditation.

Meditation promotes sustained positivity and a sense of contentment. Indeed, in the contemporary era, experiencing happiness has become an indulgence that eludes a significant portion of the populace, including individuals of considerable wealth and influence. Therefore, should you have the capacity to derive pleasure from the experiences and circumstances of life, perspicaciously comprehend that you have indeed accomplished an impressive feat. By adopting a optimistic demeanor, you will be able to derive maximum satisfaction from your life and simultaneously cultivate an understanding that joy and sadness are inevitable facets of existence, over which we possess limited power. Our course of action should be to endeavor to maintain a state of contentment to the best of our ability. Hence, the practice of meditation enables individuals to cultivate an acceptance of life's inherent fluctuations, thereby offering a means to alleviate the persistent stress one encounters.

Consequently, the practice of meditation contributes to one's state of contentment and joyfulness.

Meditation facilitates optimal concentration on tasks, thus diminishing the perceived magnitude of problems. In reality, they are actually smaller than we perceive them to be, due to the perpetual inundation of distractions we encounter on a daily basis. Hence, through the practice of meditation, the mind becomes unburdened and one gains the realization of the trivial nature of the perceived unsolvable problem.

By meditating, your outlook towards life changes and you become a better, calmer and more creative version of yourself. The attainment of perfection is reliant upon the harmonious fusion of a cognizant intellect and boundless artistic inspiration.

Types of Meditation

"At this juncture, I am confident that you are fully aware:

• What is meditation?

• What are the advantages of engaging in meditation? • What are the positive outcomes of incorporating meditation into one's routine? • How does practicing meditation contribute to one's well-being and growth?

• What is the correlation between meditation and respiration, as well as meditation and body positioning?

• If meditation is considered to be a religious practice

However, if you have conducted further investigations, you might have observed that there exist distinct variations of meditation and diverse methodologies for engaging in meditative practice. Notwithstanding the extensive array of information accessible, a substantial portion of it presents contradicting viewpoints.

Primarily, perplexity ensues due to the existence of numerous meditation techniques that vary across sources, often making it challenging to discern any differentiating factors. Just to provide you with some insight, it is important to note that there exist a vast array of meditation techniques, numbering in the hundreds if not thousands. Fortunately, among these options, there are a few notable ones that can be readily recognized and are widely favored. Additionally, divergent information regarding the suggested incorporation of specific forms of meditation for distinct groups of individuals can be obtained. For instance, in accordance with individual dispositions.

Indeed, within the confines of this particular section, we shall abstain from delineating the optimal form of meditation, as our intention is to engender further debate. To determine the most suitable form of meditation for oneself, it is advisable to experiment with various types in order to ascertain one's capability and achieve the desired outcomes. If a particular style of meditation proves effective during a certain period of one's life, then that becomes the most suitable one for the individual.

Please refrain from erroneously assuming that meditation disciplines are determined by the various meditation positions. Different types of meditation are classified based on various factors, with posture being among them.

Classification of meditation

Based on the findings of researchers, meditation can be categorized according to the manner in which attention is directed.

As a consequence, three categories of meditations arise:

- Directed focus: employing these methodologies entails maintaining exclusive attention on a solitary entity throughout the duration of the session.

The object may encompass various forms, such as visualization, mantra repetition, meditation on an external object, or focusing attention on a specific part of the body. Some illustrations consist of Samatha Meditation, Sound meditation, Loving-kindness meditation, Chakra Meditation, Mantra Meditation, Kundalini meditation, among others.

- Unrestricted observation: within this classification, the attention is directed towards any experience without constraint, while refraining from forming judgment or emotional attachment towards any particular object or action. Remain vigilant for any occurrences, auditory stimuli, olfactory sensations, tactile experiences, or recollections, permitting them to transition to the next moment. Some instances encompass Vipassana,

Mindfulness, and various forms of Taoist meditation.

• Nonchalant presence: within this classification, attention is not directed towards any particular aspect, but rather leans on its own essence. (Steady. Devoid of activity, tranquil, and introspective; it pertains to the practice of choiceless awareness or attaining a state of pure existence. Curiously, this serves as the underlying objective of all forms of meditation, although it does not exclusively align with any singular type of meditation. In certain forms of meditation, it serves as the fundamental objective throughout the entirety of the practice. For example self-enquiry meditation.

An alternative classification pertains to the various forms of meditation that have emerged from the religious traditions of Christianity, Hinduism, and Buddhism. Within this categorization, there exist five distinct classifications:

Some examples of concentration meditation techniques include Zen meditation, Om meditation, chakra meditation, transcendental meditation, and more.

- Mindfulness: instances of meditation techniques falling under this classification encompass walking meditation, seated meditation, mindful consumption, visualized meditation, body scan meditation, and deep breathing meditation.

- Innovative contemplation: commonly known as visualization, this practice aims to enhance and foster particular mental attributes.

- Centered on the heart: its purpose is to facilitate the release of all sentiments of sadness and fear, enabling individuals to embrace the virtues of compassion and kindness.

- Reflective: commonly known as contemplative meditation. It pertains to the act of selecting a theme, query, or focal point and devoting one's complete attention to scrutinizing or deliberating upon it.

Mindfulness meditation

Mindfulness meditation ranks among the most formidable contemplative practices. The primary focus lies in the meditator's endeavor to foster and nurture a profoundly receptive state of mind, directing their attention towards an object or activity within their vicinity. It cultivates mindfulness through the practice of paying deliberate attention. It demonstrates optimal efficacy in alleviating pain, promoting recovery from depression and anxiety. Whilst the practitioner engages in the act of observation, it is imperative that they maintain a detached stance towards their thoughts, refraining from any form of involvement or value-based assessment. The practitioner should solely adhere to their presence and absence.

How to accomplish the task

• The practice of mindfulness meditation entails purposefully directing one's attention to the present moment. It involves practicing non-judgmental acceptance while attentively acknowledging his emotional states, thoughts, and sensations as they manifest and dissipate.

• In order to engage in this meditation, assume a seated position on either a chair or a cushion, ensuring that your posture remains upright so as to maintain a straight alignment of your back.

• Establishing a calm atmosphere, begin directing your attention to the rhythm of your breath while maintaining a stationary posture. As an illustration, direct your attention to the inhalation and exhalation of air. An alternative phrasing in a more formal tone could be: "An additional aspect on which you may direct your attention pertains to your cognitive processes, affective experiences, and somatic sensations."

• The purpose of directing our attention to the present moment is to cultivate awareness of the events taking place in our surroundings without becoming entangled or lost in them. This practice involves deliberately channeling our mental faculties towards the specific thoughts we choose to engage with, while actively dismissing any extraneous distractions attempting to infiltrate our mind.

Mindfulness is the optimal form of meditation for novice practitioners, as it boasts a straightforward acquisition and execution process. Furthermore, this particular style of meditation is commonly imparted in numerous healthcare facilities, educational institutions, and residential environments. While its roots can be traced back to Buddhist meditation, this practice is accessible to individuals of all backgrounds and can be pursued independently of religious affiliations without generating any conflicts. Furthermore, it has been determined that this particular option garners the highest favorability among individuals seeking both psychological and physical advantages.

How To Meditate?

To engage in the practice of meditation, one must achieve a state of relaxation, direct their attention to a singular point of focus, and diligently return to it whenever their attention wavers. You are allowed to engage in meditation for any duration of your choosing, be it as brief as 3 minutes or as extensive as you desire. In order to enhance your meditation proficiency, it is advisable to progressively extend the duration of each session.

It is within your discretion to choose whether or not to monitor the duration of your meditation practice. In the event that you choose to do so, kindly establish an alarm with a low volume to prevent any abrupt disturbance upon awakening from the hypnotic state. You are also welcome to conclude the session at your discretion when you believe it is appropriate to do so.

There exist meditation practices that require stillness, as well as those that incorporate movement. The following techniques are as follows:

Cultivating Mindfulness

Mindfulness entails maintaining a state of heightened awareness and attentiveness to the present moment's unfolding events. Allow your consciousness to operate at its optimum level. Take note of the occurrences in your physical, mental, and surrounding domains. Merely engage in observation without indulging in prolonged contemplation. Refain from contemplating the future, past, or any matter of concern. In the event that a thought arises within your consciousness, it is advisable to internally acknowledge it as "A thought", while subsequently redirecting your attention towards maintaining a state of focus. Do not conceal your consciousness beneath a cascade of contemplations.

This is relevant and applicable both during and outside the practice of meditation. Refrain from continuously passing judgement on individuals, objects, concepts, and circumstances. Do not allow your preconceived notions and past encounters to hinder your current encounter. Make an effort to apprehend the current state of reality as it truly exists, without the influence of your recollections or anticipations.

One's perception often becomes constrained by their deeply-held beliefs. Take a moment to still your thoughts, allowing your consciousness to wander without constraint. Engaging in such behavior yields a novel viewpoint, facilitates the accomplishment of additional tasks, and promotes liberation from cognitive routines.

Sensing a Target

Enhancing your sense of awareness towards a specific objective can heighten your state of mindfulness. Select a material that is aesthetically pleasing to you, such as fabric, beads, a pebble, or a wooden object. Examine the tactile qualities of this object. Allocate a brief interval towards this endeavor, refraining from the scrutiny or evaluation of said experience.

One can also engage in this activity by utilizing their additional senses; for instance, by visually examining the various hues and shades exhibited by a flower, or by attentively listening to the vibrant melodies and rhythms produced by a bird or musical piece. Examine your perception of the world. Make an effort to not disregard anything solely on the basis of its commonplace nature. One will become aware of various aspects that are often overlooked and thus it is advisable to employ complete attentiveness whenever possible.

Stopping and Sensing

Establish a timed notification or request the assistance of an acquaintance to interject at unpredictable intervals, particularly when engrossed in a habitual undertaking. Cease all current activities and direct your full attention to the physical sensations you are experiencing, including but not limited to pressure, sense of equilibrium, textures, and temperatures.

Walking Meditation

While taking a stroll, refrain from becoming engrossed in your own musings, and instead, take in your surroundings. Observe how your cognition attempts to divert your attention from immediate perception by constructing judgments regarding the phenomena you are presently observing. Refuse to yield to the allure of your thoughts until you have completed the walking meditation.

Move at a leisurely pace, exhibiting deliberate intent. Take notice of the motion generated by your upper and lower extremities. Devote diligent observation to one's surroundings without conscious consideration. Divert your attention from your concerns. Remain mindful of your breath and keenly observe all discernible sensations while in motion.

Self-Commentary

Engage in a cognitive evaluation of your actions in real-time. For instance, consider the following scenarios:

"Currently, I am engrossed in reading this book." "At present, I am hydrating myself by taking a sip of water." "In the present moment, I am contemplating my future meal choices." "I am presently returning to my book, after a brief interruption." Adhering to this practice will effectively anchor your experiences in your mind, thereby preventing any lapse in concentration. It is possible to readily recollect one's activities at a later point in time.

Daily Review

Prior to retiring for the night, engage in a deliberate recollection of the occurrences and experiences that transpired throughout the course of the day. You have the choice to consider them in a sequential manner or in any preferred sequential order. Are there any omissions or discrepancies in the chronology of today's events? In which possible direction is your mental focus directed during those intervals? Develop a strategy to mitigate future distractions.

Breathing meditation

Numerous cultural customs associate the act of respiration with the practice of meditation. Regulating your respiration empowers you to govern your emotional experiences. By engaging in slow and deliberate respiration, one can effectively decelerate their heart rate and induce a state of tranquility.

Practicing breath-focused meditation entails directing your awareness towards your breath and/or engaging in deliberate breathing techniques. When you engage in diaphragmatic breathing, you are allowing your breath to originate from the abdomen rather than the chest or upper torso. Utilizing diaphragmatic breathing facilitates the intake of up to tenfold greater amounts of oxygen into the body compared to chest breathing.

In order to determine if you are utilizing diaphragmatic breathing, kindly position one hand upon your chest and the other onto your abdomen. The movement of the hand placed on your abdomen should be more pronounced compared to the one resting on your chest.

Refrain from engaging in deep inhalations, instead, maintain a natural rhythm of respiration. Breathe quietly and easily. During the act of respiration, it is advised to direct your focus towards the area below your nose, where one can discern the ingress and egress of air. Direct your attention to your breath and quietly perceive the sensations without engaging in internal dialogue.

Respiratory regulation entails the process of inhaling, retaining the breath, and subsequently exhaling. A frequently utilized method of regulating respiration is known as the two-for-one breathing technique. This implies a breath-out duration that is twice the length of your inhalation.

Inhale steadily and profoundly through your nostrils, while sequentially counting to four. Ensure that the abdomen expands while the chest remains stationary. Please refrain from inhaling while mentally reciting the numbers, 1, 2, 3, 4. Engage in a deliberate and controlled exhalation through your nasal passages, ensuring that it is carried out gradually and without interruption. While doing so, proceed to mentally enumerate the numbers 1, 2, 3, 4, 5, 6, 7, 8. Sustain the suspension of your breath for an additional four counts. Perform this action consecutively for a maximum of 10 iterations.

Should you discover that the duration of the counts is excessive, it is permissible to abbreviate them; nevertheless, endeavor to ensure that the length of your exhalations exceeds that of your inhalations. Please proceed in a slow and measured manner, ensuring that you maintain a comfortable rhythm. Please proceed with this action for a few minutes.

Slowing down the exhalation process has the potential to diminish the neuronal activity in your brain and induce a state of tranquility in your mind. This proves particularly advantageous, particularly in instances of anger or anxiety. Anxiety and anger trigger the fight-or-flight response; employing this breathing technique will counteract the impact and assist in restoring your composure.

Heartbeat Meditation

Place your hand atop your chest or perceive the rhythm of your heartbeat. Take heed of your heart rate - you have the option to tally each individual beat if you so desire. Continue performing this action for a duration of approximately three minutes.

Using Objects

Maintain a subdued lighting ambiance while ensuring sufficient brightness to allow for clear visibility of your intended subject. Position your image or object at a height that aligns with the line of sight, ensuring a suitable distance from your meditation space. Kindly shut your eyes and transition into a state of meditation. Ensure that your vision is fully attentive and fixate it directly onto your intended objective. Only blink when it is necessary. Please make an effort to maintain steadiness in your gaze. Redirect your gaze to a singular focal point within the image and refrain from being distracted by other elements or objects.

Refrain from decrypting or assessing the subject, as this will merely disperse your attention. Allow the object to direct your focus. Acknowledge that the item is situated both before you and within the confines of your thoughts. When one engages in the contemplation of a significant symbol, such as a mandala, the associated meaning profoundly influences the depths of the subconscious. There is no need for you to ruminate upon it.

Musical Meditation

One may engage in meditation while incorporating music in the background, yet the music can function as the focal point of the meditation itself. You carefully attend to the music and willingly yield to its influence, allowing it to transport you. The crucial aspect lies in embracing the experience rather than distancing oneself from it through a layer of reflections.

Problem Solving with Meditation

During the course of your meditation, you have the opportunity to address and resolve the issue at hand. Please be advised that when you are in a meditative state, you possess a heightened level of mental control, thereby enabling you to more effectively solve problems.

Meditative Yoga Poses

Now, one might query the connection between yoga and mindfulness meditation. By engaging in yoga practice, individuals can reap the advantages of integrating physical movements with mindfulness, resulting in a transformative and unparalleled experience. It is imperative to refrain from disregarding the physical aspects as a trivial concern, as the integration of the mind and body is fundamental, and their optimal functioning is mutually dependent. According to a research conducted by Dr. Shealy, the amalgamation of yoga and meditation stimulates our inherent capacity for self-healing. It harnesses our capacity to nurture self-compassion and embodied wisdom, thereby imparting valuable lessons on embracing the present moment and confronting any challenges with a mindset characterized by sincerity, clarity, and ethical authenticity.

Practice Tips

Mindful yoga exemplifies a form of kinetic meditation, wherein I present to you a set of key aspects upon which to direct your attention, fostering a steadfast presence of mind.

Breath

Throughout the duration of the yoga practice, it is important to maintain a heightened awareness of your breath. Inspect it to verify its coherence, smoothness, and cadence. It is advisable to maintain a consistent pattern of both exhalations and inhalations. Effective breath control holds significant importance within the practice of yoga, as it aids in mitigating post-exercise muscle soreness. Additionally, directing your attention towards your breath will assist in centering your thoughts on the present moment, preventing them from straying.

Transitions

As you transition between different yoga postures, it is advisable to maintain a mindful awareness of your body's movements. Direct your attention towards the sensations originating from the skeletal and muscular systems.

Sense of Grounding

While performing each yoga posture, strive to evaluate the specific body region that is making contact with the ground. To develop strength or involve your entire body, you can exert active force upon the body parts that make contact with the ground, pressing them in opposition to the floor.

Spine

For every pose in which you engage, endeavor to inquire within yourself regarding the position and alignment of your spinal column. Consistency is imperative, whereby the response to each inquiry ought to remain unchanged; it should be an extension.

Warm Up Exercise

Prior to commencing any yoga meditation exercise, it is imperative that you engage in a warm-up routine lasting no less than one to two minutes. Commence by assuming a mountain pose, characterized by the posture of standing upright without deviation. Position both of your hands at the central region of your chest, assuming an anatomical posture reminiscent of a prayer gesture. Gently elevate both of your hands while breathing in, and as you breathe out, return them to their initial position.

10-Minute Yoga Exercise

Prior to commencing this round, kindly engage in appropriate warm-up exercises. Commence by sequentially performing the following yoga exercises for a total of four rounds. Every cycle would entail performing the exercise on the left as well as the right side. During the initial round, it is recommended to maintain the yoga pose for a minimum of 5 or 6 complete breath cycles, equivalent to approximately 30 seconds. Subsequently, for the second and third rounds, the duration should be reduced to 2 breath cycles, approximately 10 to 12 seconds each. During the final round, it is advised to maintain each yoga pose for a single breath, which equates to approximately 5 seconds.

High Lunge

As you have recently completed the warm-up with a mountain pose, commence the high lunge by subsequently displacing your right foot to the rear, at a distance of approximately two to three feet, while elevating your heel off the ground. Please exercise caution during the transition. As you flex your left knee in adjustment, exhale while elevating your arms directly above your head, ensuring they remain parallel without intertwining. Maintain a position in which your thigh remains as parallel to the floor as possible, while exerting pressure on both feet in order to achieve and sustain equilibrium. Subsequently, subsequent to the specified duration of maintaining this posture, reposition your right foot in line with your left foot and proceed to assume the mountain pose again, with your arms resting gracefully at your sides as you inhale.

Warrior Pose II

From the position of mountain pose, proceed to move your right foot rearwards and establish a solid footing on the ground, ensuring a 90-degree angle between your right foot and your left foot. Simultaneously, gracefully lower your left knee whilst maintaining a parallel alignment with the floor.

Rotate your body sideways and direct your head towards the same direction as your left foot. Stretch out your arms, resembling the form of an aircraft, aligned in a parallel position to your shoulders. Please refrain from both leaning forward and arching your back, and instead focus on maintaining proper spinal alignment. Resume the mountain pose and perform the exercise once more in a mirrored fashion.

Reverse Warrior

Transitioning from the mountain pose, assume a warrior pose II by aligning your left arm with the extended left leg, avoiding any exerted pressure, while simultaneously extending your right arm upwards and reaching backward. As you move from the Warrior Pose II to the Reverse Warrior, notice the activation of your posterior muscles. As you inhale, transition back into warrior pose II and ascend to mountain pose before proceeding with the same sequence on the opposite side.

Humble Warrior

Transition into a warrior pose II by assuming a position where your hands are interlocked behind your back. Practice controlled breathing while gradually lowering your shoulder and chest towards the inner side of your knee, simultaneously engaging your leg muscles. Subsequently, gradually extend your arms above your head, perceiving the consequent opening of your shoulders and chest. As you elevate your chest, take a deep breath in, and upon untangling your hands, exhale while transitioning back into warrior pose II. Resume the mountain pose and proceed to execute the pose once more, alternating to the opposite side.

After completing the four rounds, it is advised to reiterate the warm-up exercise for an additional duration of one to two minutes prior to concluding your session.

20-Minute Yoga Meditation

In a manner similar to any other yoga regimen, initiate this 20-minute exercise by engaging in a warm-up lasting one to two minutes. Subsequently, perform three iterations of the aforementioned sequential yoga regimen. Similar to the 10-minute exercise, every iteration would involve performing the pose on both the left and right sides. In round 1, it is recommended to maintain each pose for a duration of 5 to 6 breaths, while in round 2, the suggested timeframe is 2 breaths per pose, and finally, in round 3, it is advised to hold each pose for a single breath. After mastering the poses, you have the option to incorporate an additional round into your routine, thus extending your exercise session to a duration of 20 minutes.

Initiate the sequence by assuming a High Lunge posture, followed by transitioning into Warrior Pose II, Reverse Warrior, and concluding with Humble Warrior, mirroring the asana progression observed within the aforementioned 10-minute Yoga meditation session. Subsequently, proceed to perform these subsequent yoga postures in a orderly succession.

Tree Pose (Variation)

Commencing from the mountain stance, transfer your body's weight onto your left foot. Elevate your right foot, directing it towards your left upper thigh, while maintaining a vertical position with the sole of your left foot facing upwards as you take a breath inward. Given that this pose is a modified version of the tree pose designed to accommodate beginners in yoga, it is recommended to maintain balance by grasping your left toes with your left hand. Next, assume a hand posture reminiscent of prayer by placing your right hand in the corresponding position. Please pay attention to the key areas of focus and take a deep breath in order to elongate the spine. Revert to the mountain pose and perform the asana on the opposite side.

Warrior Pose III

Transitioning from Mountain Pose, transfer your body's weight onto your right leg while gently positioning your left leg behind you at a distance of no more than one foot, ensuring only a light contact of your toes with the ground. Inhale deeply, while keeping your spine aligned, gently tilt your torso forward. While lifting your left leg, simultaneously extend your arms forward to establish alignment between your arms, back, and leg. Please ensure that you are conscious of your movement technique and maintaining proper posture for your spine. Please assume mountain pose once again and proceed to repeat the pose on the opposite side.

Pose of the Dance Leader

Commence by transferring your body weight onto your right foot and flexing the left knee, simultaneously extending the left arm towards the rear in order to secure a hold on the left foot. In order to generate the necessary traction, it is recommended that you elevate your leg and chest more prominently by exerting pressure from your foot onto your hand. If it becomes requisite to attain equilibrium, you may adopt a forward-leaning position. Contract the quadriceps to provide stability to your right foot. Direct your attention a few feet ahead of your current position, fixating on a specific point while extending your right hand in that same direction. Engage in contemplation of the salient aspects while inhaling and exhaling. Gradually assume the mountain pose again and proceed to repeat this posture on the opposite side.

Low Lunge

While maintaining focused gaze on a point ahead, proceed to flex your left knee, gradually descending your right leg in a rearward motion. Please execute this task discreetly. Permit your left knee to make contact with the floor, while simultaneously extending your arms upward and aligning them alongside your ears, ensuring not to interlace your fingers. Elevate the sternum and align your chest as you elevate the lower abdomen while exerting pressure on your leading foot. It is imperative that you remember to engage in deep breaths and engage in focused meditation on the central aspects. Please revert to the mountain pose and proceed to replicate the pose on the opposite side.

Prior to concluding your yoga mindfulness practice, conclude your regimen with a period of one to two minutes dedicated to the warm-up exercise.

www.ingramcontent.com/pod-product-compliance
Lightning Source LLC
Chambersburg PA
CBHW050413120526
44590CB00015B/1951